Mim and Tim

By Debbie Croft

Mim sits at the pit.

Tim sips at the tap.

The mat.

Is Mim at the mat?

Is Mim at the tap?

Is Mim at the mat?

Tim!

Mim is at the pit.

CHECKING FOR MEANING

1. What is Tim doing at the start of the story? *(Literal)*

2. Where does Tim find Mim? *(Literal)*

3. What do you think Mim was doing in the pit? *(Inferential)*

EXTENDING VOCABULARY

sits	Look at the word *sits*. What is the base of this word? What has been added to the base? What other word in the book has an *s* added to the base?
mat	Look at the word *mat*. How many sounds are in *mat*? How many letters? What other words do you know that start with the same sound as *mat*?
Mim	Look at the word *Mim*. Why does it always start with a capital letter? What other words or names do you know that always start with a capital letter?

MOVING BEYOND THE TEXT

1. Do you think Mim and Tim had a good time at the gym?

2. What activities can people do at the gym?

3. What else can you do to stay fit?

4. What is your favourite way to exercise?

SPEED SOUNDS

Mm	Ss	Aa	Pp	Ii	Tt

PRACTICE WORDS

Mim

at

sits

pit

sips

Tim

mat

tap

Sit